THE GRAVITY INSIDE US

THE GRAVITY INSIDE US

poetry and prose

Chloë Frayne

THE GRAVITY INSIDE US

Andrews McMeel Publishing
a division of Andrews McMeel Universal
1130 Walnut Street, Kansas City, Missouri 64106

www.andrewsmcmeel.com

21 22 23 24 25 VEP 10 9 8 7 6 5 4 3 2 1

ISBN: 978-1-5248-6324-1

Library of Congress Control Number: 2020945203

Cover art by Amanda C. Marino

Editor: Patty Rice
Art Director/Designer: Tiffany Meairs
Production Editor: Elizabeth A. Garcia
Production Manager: Carol Coe

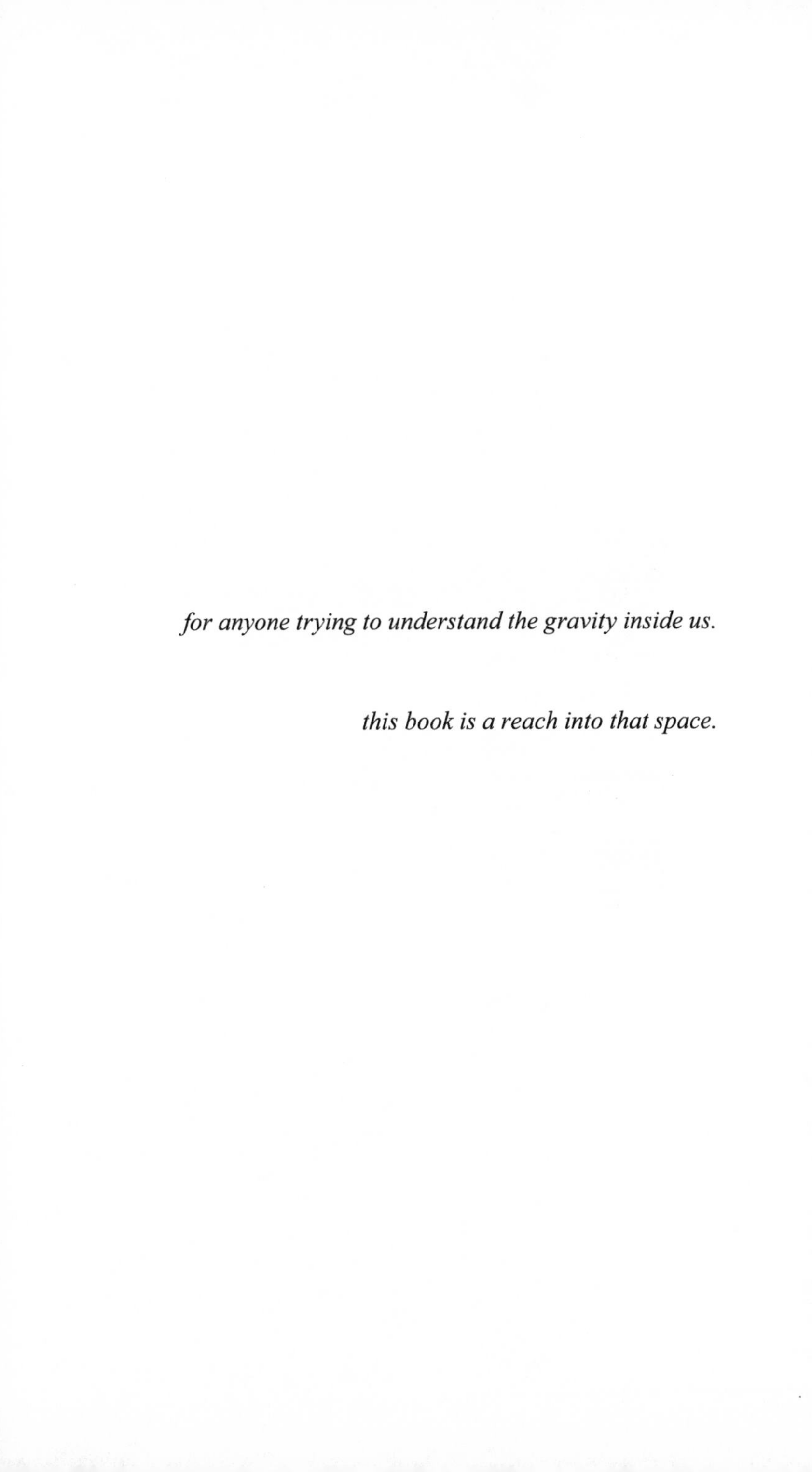

for anyone trying to understand the gravity inside us.

this book is a reach into that space.

I once read an article about the
electromagnetic energy of a heart. a scientist
had discovered that one heart could feel another
from three feet away. a pulse.

I began to develop a theory about gravity.

it stands to reason that if there is something
inside us that reaches
for the thing inside someone else,
we have begun to understand
the science of fate.
it stands to reason that, if we call this a gravity,
people pull us more than planets.

chapters

a beckoning

hope. wanderlust. the pull.

There is a gravity
inside us,
don't you think?

A pull.
An undeniability.
A falling into place.

A quiet understanding
in the way
I see you
and the ocean makes sense.
A moon falling into orbit makes sense.
The way the universe
is held together
makes sense.

I hope
the light
is finding you
even (especially)
when you do not
have the strength
to go
looking for it.

I want to be
a field
of wildflowers,
constantly claiming
new ground.

And what is this
of freedom?
How does this taste
like clean air?

Let this be an act of courage.
Let this brush the dust
from your weary breath.
Let this strike a match
against your bones.
Let this small romance
bloom madly
against your skin.

Let this be
the way we begin.

I press hope against my palms
like a flower between pages,
like a prayer.
It is quietly defiant,
a soft whisper in a safe place
and, yet,
a match thrown against a flame.
It licks across my skin
and speaks of rebirth
and wildfire.
I hold my hand against the sky
and it is a miracle to feel at all.

I am afraid more
than I'd like to admit.
but
this is a call for courage;
this is nothing
but an opportunity
for an uprising.

I want to tell you a story about bravery.
I want you to forget every over-romanticized notion
you've ever heard about fearlessness;
replace it with the idea that bravery is not an absence of fear
but a rebellion against it.
that it's taking the risk. reaching
for the person you want. chasing your dream.
fighting for it all (despite despite despite).
Bravery is hoping it's worth it.
Stop holding your humanity like a failure
and wondering why you can't succeed.
Fear is an instinct to keep us safe and alive—
it's healthy to carry it as long as you don't allow it
to control you. Perpetuating the idea
that we can scrape it from us completely
only serves to breed more fear, make us feel alone,
and create shame for something that exists
(and should exist) in every breathing thing.
Make no mistake: everyone is afraid of something.
Everyone is taking a risk, in their own way.
Every day, people are finding their dreams.
surviving. falling in love. letting go.
moving forward. stepping back. staying. healing.
Every single one of them is doing so despite the fear, not without it.

Set your sights on what you genuinely want and not just what is easy.
Hold hope with both hands. be afraid. jump anyway.

What I'm trying to tell you is:
don't aspire to be fearless. aspire to be brave.

I think if you have a chance—
even a chance—
at your dream,
it's a sin
if you don't take it.

If you won't fight
for what you want,
you can't be surprised
when someone else
gets it.

whatever happens,
I'll go with you.

Do not settle
for what you have
when your heart knows
exactly what you want.

Build a home in the place
you daydream of.
Build it with the person
you dreamed
was standing beside you.

Be the architect
of your own damn life.

Most of the relationships I've had or wanted
have been with women who talked about
these big, beautiful futures with me
with little to no intention of having them.
people who wanted me one day, and not the next.
people who cheated on me, or emotionally abused me,
or didn't try at all.

Sometimes when I think about the way I loved them,
I get so scared that the trauma and grief they left me with
will make it harder or impossible
for me to ever feel that way again
and the possibility of that breaks my heart.
but, listen.
Imagine how much I will love someone
who means what they say; who buries hope in my hands
out of more than curiosity.
who reaches for me without wishing I were someone else
and touches me without it feeling like an echo.
who can't imagine a future without me in it.

Imagine the stories I will write about them.

This life is unfolding.
It has been a closed bud;
a falling wave; a fist held tight
around hope; a house boarded shut
for too long. The air is stale.
We heal enough to open a window
And, suddenly, there is fresh air.

Hope floods in and
we breathe without apology.

The doors slowly open
and it uncurls inside you:
the possibility.

the idea
that just maybe

there's
a place
for me.

I called you
an unmet adventure
like maybe you could be
the greatest one yet.

and, see?—
how
contagiously alive
you are; how
intimately tied
to oblivion.

A soft desire

to be wanted
in such a way
that
it does not
build a home
for doubt.

If a mind is a museum,
we must curate it.
decide
how big the monument is.
chronicle our battles.
honor our victories in halls.
pin and stuff and mount
our losses along walls.
tell visitors what it was like
in the past.
paint pictures.
stand them in clusters and explain
the nature of stars.
look at every room in the building carefully
and build a new wing for our dreams.
fill it and fill it and fill it
with possibilities.

Maybe it all comes down
to that moment of hesitation
as I reach for my car door.
to the way that sometimes
I drive past my house
five times
before I pull in the driveway.
to that breath I take
before "I love you."

Maybe I still
haven't figured out
where I want to be.

The clouds have settled against the sky.
The sun will soon tuck itself away
for the night and, still, I think
I am not ready.
The world seems to fall into its place,
and as hard as I have tried,
I have not found my way.
I have curled myself into places
that never should have known my shape;
wrapped myself in the arms of strangers
and felt nothing
but flight. but fear. but
knowing it is not enough.
Because how can you build homes
in dangerous lands?—
if the sky is on fire
and the earth never stands still
and you cannot seem to learn
to stop falling?—
if you have waited
(and waited and waited)
to be caught before you hit rock bottom
and, still, found yourself
crawling up the cliff alone?

I want adventure
to flower
against my skin
like war paint.

I want to fight
for my life.

I hope you see that
even on my best days
I dream about
running away.

(I hope you see how
hard I have tried
to wrap my hands
around the word
enough.)

And I hope when
the time comes,
you won't
hold it against me
for leaving.
The way I won't
hold it against you
for needing to stay.

Do you see?—
miles pour across miles
like the scattering
of stars
and, still,
I am not afraid.

(and I think
this is softness;
this is strength.)

I don't mean to say
I need just one more reason to stay,

but it comes out anyway.

I imagine that,
somewhere in the world,
you are breathing sunlit air;
growing and learning how
to bloom again.
Healing has become
second nature
in a way that
most people
will never understand.

and for this girl,
I have an immeasurable patience.
an infinite hope.

A flock of migrating birds passed over the house today
and, almost instinctively, I felt something in the distance
calling me away. The solstice had come and gone
and I had already been struggling to stay,
but, with this, there is promise
of hope.

A feather winds its way to the earth
and, like a checkered flag, I pack my bags.

I am a ship against the tide;
sails full of sea breeze.
I am nothing but a bird;
eyes fixed on the sky.

In this version of the story,
I let myself be happy

and I never
(not once)
let you make me feel bad about it.

It’s not that I loved you—
not that I was even stumbling.
but I looked at you
and saw tied-together shoelaces
on too-big shoes
standing on the precipice
of fly or fall.

I looked at you
and knew that I could.

A lot goes on
behind closed doors.

(like how we slam them.
like how we stand
on the other side
with pressed backs
and closed fists
and closed eyes
and pray
for the courage
to open them.)

You must understand, I have never known
how to be something that does not scare you.
I am too many words, wrapped in something
that has seen more wars and softness
than you could bear to look at.
To your credit, I know you tried.
I know your gaze brushed across my skin
and tried to find a home.
I will not hold it against you
for only seeing bomb shelters.
I know you have carried swords for so long
that your heart became a shield and
you have lowered it enough times
for me to understand that you are not ready
to surrender.
I reach for you and there are no white flags.
I tell you I want to be with you
and you look at me like
I am a bomb, dropping.

We are unshakable.
We hold hands and
the earth stands still.
We build kingdoms
and homes
and hopes
on solid ground
and, for once,
we are not afraid.

and then we feel
the tremor.

They look at my hands and see fault lines;
trace their fingers along one and
tell me how I should have known better.
Quietly note their length across my palms; say,
"It's right here, don't you see?—
there were pockets full of red flags
and you were too busy writing poems
about the beautiful things
to notice."

I tell them that
love has never blinded me.
I will not apologize for
the people I have wanted.
Don't you understand?—

I see fault lines in my hands
and *I should have known better,*
but
hope is an earthquake.

and I just keep falling.

I thought of
all the things
I wanted
to say to you

and I swallowed
a sea.

Someone asks me
when I will date again,
and
without hesitating,
I say,
"When her laugh
is no longer
my favorite sound
in the world."

There is a secret to beginning to heal.
listen close:
stop trying to get back to the person you were before.
before the love. before the hurt. before
it felt like your life was crumbling around you
and all you could do was keep breathing.
before love set your world on fire.
before grief burned it down.
before you lost whatever you thought about
when you read the first line.
you are not the same person you were before this.
you never will be again.
it's okay if you need to grieve that, but, whatever you do,
please celebrate it, too.
you were loved even if you didn't get to keep it.
you were held even if someone let go.
you have grown no matter how hard it has been.
you held a light in your hands, and by some miracle
it found its way to your heart.
you are a new version of yourself. a new chapter. a new phase.
you are overflowing with possibility.
I hope you believe this.
I hope you take these lessons as a gift for your future
and know you are moving forward
with a better understanding of your head and heart
and what they need. you may have lost something you wanted,
but now you will choose something that's a little more right for you.
a new beginning with a better chance of a happy end.

I'm proud of the person you are now.

I hope you are, too.

I have remained
petal-soft
through the winter
of heartbreak.

despite this new season. despite
every piece of advice I was given.
I did not run. grow hard or selfish.
I did not build walls out of fear.
I lost but remained.
I grew taller. stronger. waited for the spring.
and I am still almost unbearably soft;
still me.

My next love will require more patience than my last ever had.

This is the nature of heartbreak.
I hold the softness of my heart with both hands
and I think about healing.
how many days (weeks) (months)
it devoured with grief
and without apology.
how slowly feeling anything is coming back to life.

I gather every ounce of grace
and thank my heart for not hardening.
thank it for the miracle it is
to find joy in a new smile.
new hands. someone else's voice in the dark.

I will regift names. try to find new ones.
call her "baby" with a little more comfort each time.
it doesn't feel like your name anymore, but, still,
it used to be.
that is an echo; everything is a new sound.
I tell everyone who will listen
that healing is slow, hard work.
I tell them how tender this heart still is.
I beg them to be patient.
I tell them I will fall in love again.
this time, it will be slow. purposeful.
only with the gathering certainty
that, this time,
she will catch me.

Perhaps it is naive
to promise you that
I will never leave you
in some capacity,
but I can promise you
at least this:

I will never leave you
with a head
full of questions
and no one
to answer them.

I have always been attracted
to artists and tattoos.

There is just something
so damn beautiful
about a person
unafraid
of forever.

If you keep me
in your heart
beside
deleted texts,
nervously given compliments,
and love letters
tucked and hidden
in the very back corner
of your bottom drawer,
then
let me go.

I will not be
your secret.

Do not reach for me
with
someone else's name
on your breath;
with
indecision on your hands.
I am
an Always.
do you understand?
I am
a new language.

When I was with you,
music lived in everything.
The world woke up around me
and raised its voice
to the stars.

I am no less of a person
when I am not in love,
but I walk down the street now
and it is much less
of a symphony.

I am still searching
for an earth
that holds me
more
than the sky.

What I mean to say is,
I can't grow in your hands.

Love me like that
stupid Christmas feeling.
like maybe one day
when we're old
and time has turned all our pages,
you might look up at me
on Christmas morning
and think how
it's still magic.

I hold a dream like sunlight inside me.
It took eleven years to come true, but I never let it go.

Maybe that's the secret to all of this—
to let hope inspire you to have the courage
to dream again. to find what's good for you—
what's right for you—and even in this chaos
(especially in this chaos)
never let it go.

Here is something I have said
more times than I can count:
I am too patient. I give too many chances.
I could line up every person in my life
and they would tell you the same thing.
I have made more jokes about it than they have.
I have misplaced this gift of patience
(of second chances)
often.
We joke about that, too.
But I have never thought less of myself for it.

Someday, there will be someone in my life
who needs more chances
than other people know how to give them.
who requires patience.
I will have the capacity to love them.
For that person, I will be
exactly the right amount of grace.

We look at an aspect of ourselves
in a moment of our lives,
and we say, "This does not fit,"
without so much as questioning
whether it is simply not its time.

The rest of your life is a long time;
everything inside you will have its place,
even if it is not understood today.

When they ask you
about the poems,
tell them
this one
was for you.

Somewhere
between fear
and courage,

I allow myself
enough grace
to dream
about you.

I write books about
what it is to be in love
and you smile like
you are not afraid
I might write about you.

Branches weave above you
like fingers
against the sun
and I look at you
and
a miracle
has begun.

There is your smile

and it is
a light. a flicker.
something that looks
so much
like hope.

I want to write poetry with you.
I want your laugh
to stir books inside me;
I want to catch it
in my lungs.
I want the night to bear down,
heavy-lidded,
thick with summer,
and hotly breathe
words
against your skin.
Which is to say,
I want to know you
the way the sky does.
Which is to say,
your fingers close
around letters
and I think
you have always been
a song.

At best,
I hope I can be
a reawakening of joy.

At least,
I hope I can
hold your hand.

Hope looks like
a girl smiling at me on a sunlit street.
green eyes and a collection of rings.
an arm wrapped around me.
quietly. like maybe we are
the only two people who notice.
but we're not. because

Hope looks like
an old lady, hands clasped.
the way you pull through thrift store aisles.
look up. see me. say
I look beautiful.
touch my face like it is something familiar.

I reach for your hand and
I am telling you,
this is hope.

I want to be
more to you
than
just a chance
you didn't take.

She looks up
and smiles at me
and, suddenly,
fear
is not
a second language
but something
that is crushed
against the ground
between us.

If I imagine
the women who have held me
and I think too long about
the hardness of their hands,
I almost let go of yours.
I almost abandon the idea
of bravery. the sweet gentle of
your skin against mine.

I think someday I will look back on this time
and not be able to explain it without saying
I was falling in love.

This is an open door.
This is you
standing on the porch.

You smile at me
like a caged bird singing
finally
on the other side of the bars
and I am so caught up
in the promise
of it all.

(You are an idea
that has run
madly, wildly
away
from
me.)

It is early
and
the light filters in like something searching.
it finds your skin.

finds the folds of sheets,
runs its fingers up the walls.
comes back to you.

completely
unmistakably
does not touch me.

and, yet,
I do not mind.

In truth, I think
my fingers will brush
beneath your eyes
and I will see
every story
I have ever wanted
to write.

I just want to know what it would feel like
to have your bones crash into me.

I think
I might always
be jealous
of the way
sunlight
touches
your skin.

People ask if I am dating
and I explain the color of her eyes
without letting her name slip between
the spaces where I have tucked it
behind my teeth.
Not because she's a secret
but
more of a birthday wish;
too soft and sacred and
probably governed by some rule book
of how to make it come true.

All I know—
all I have ever
needed to know—
is that
if you offered me
your hand,
I would take it.

As long as
our hearts
are paper
and our hands
are ink,

there will be poetry.

Don't be jealous of the way other people
have made me feel.
There is no trauma on your hands.

Which is to say,
there is still so much future
for you to claim.

Because, you?
You are made of beginnings.
You are unbridled joy,
capable of anything.
Still gathered upon the bones
of possibility.
Still feathered by the wings
of hope.

This is the story:
your hands will touch my skin
without feeling like an echo.
You will laugh and
I will think of nothing else.

The way spring
will bite through
the tail of winter;
break teeth on cold ground
when the earth
is still hard
and the birds
have not yet
begun to sing;
push and uncurl
new life
through
the last frost
with nothing
but a quiet hope
for sun.

I promise
in this way,
I have the courage
to love you.

Happiness finds me
like the breeze between buildings.
under doorways. through the spaces
sadness did not even think to close.
Once, I stood on a cliff edge
and the wind devoured me.
All I can remember is that
you held my hand.

I take the parts of me that need to be healed
and I lay them at the feet of adventure.
I pack them in suitcases.
I show them the world.
I say, "Do you see?
there is still so much left for us.
we are at the fingertips of a new life.
clean hands will hold us again someday.
we will know the touch of a new love.
there will be more joy
than the belly of heartache can imagine.
there are infinite possibilities ahead of us.

we are healing, and
this is how we fight for them."

It would be a falsehood to speak about grief,
depression, or mental health
without honoring the good days. the joy. the light.
the moments it found me.

if I tell you a story about my heart,
I want to speak of more than the breaking.
I want to tell you about the things that put me back together.
my niece's laugh. lying in my sister's arms. sleeping
between my parents. you. adventures.
a girl with her lips pressed against my scars.
planning a future with excitement again. new tattoos.
days spent with my typewriter. my best friends, by the sea.
you.

but, mostly,
me.

I want to tell you how hard I fought to be here.

I want to tell you that joy was a ghost on the horizon
and, still, I found it again.

saltwater words

distance. travel. missing you.

0.1 hertz

I sit on subway trains and think about electromagnetic energy.
I try to feel people the way I felt you.

0.1 hertz

the current of love. gratitude. kindness.
the only time
the frequency of a heart. the intelligence of emotion.
matches that of
animals. trees. the planet.
the exact moment a heartbeat drops
to meet the wave energy in someone you love.

when viewed, some neural patterns look like constellations.
a moon falls into orbit, but only with a certain planet.
no matter how far away I am
or how many people are seated around me,
none of them feel like you.

what I mean to say is,
all evidence of love
points to gravity.

I have wrapped you
safe
in summer;
and lightly, so lightly,
there is sweet August
against your skin.
Seasons, like oceans,
curl between us,
but see?—
today we are
a little closer.
The sun collapses
against the sea
and, oh,
the possibility.

bury yourself in my hair.
in my smile. in the palms of my hands.
I will carry you with me
to the ends of the earth.

I have watched the boats
sway against the sea.
I have noticed,
with great purpose,
the spaces between the stars.

What I am trying to say is that
distance is a concept
that we have given weight.
What I am trying to say is that
when it is faced with love,
it is an irrelevancy.
What I hope you understand
is that I would cross it
in any measure, to be with you.

Love, like the tide
(I never know what you mean)

Hands, like waves
(won't you wash me clean?)

Oh, distance—
what an
exquisitely
conquerable
thing.

The sea
could stretch on
forever,

but it doesn't.

Do you understand?

Sometimes
it feels selfish
to want so much
and be unable
to stay,
but every time
I take a step back
from you,
I take two steps forward
because I can't stand
how it felt.

There was something
about the way
you grabbed
my shirtfront
that the fabric
can't let go of.
I still leave
the house with
the ghost of you
tugging at my chest
while the iron
burns holes
in the board.

In my head, I play out the lives
we could have led
if you had just once
asked me to stay.

Time
stretches
between us
and it is
so much worse
than distance.

(There is nothing
I wouldn't do
to get back to you.)

I am tired of the editing;
of reining it in
and watering it down
and breaking myself
into tiny little pieces
just for you to tell me
they are still too much.
And I don't understand
because I had to work
so hard
to make them that small.

Nothing breaks my heart
like the fact
that I want to
give you an ocean
and you
are holding out
a cup.

I don't know how
to speak to you
without overflowing;
without promises
spilling
from my lungs;
without a tide
of wanting you
washed
against my skin.

And these
are saltwater words,
but I hope you are
a home
for an ocean.

I know
you are looking at me
like a window
to a world
and not
a door.

And I am begging you
to climb through,

but that is not
what windows
are for.

I let you go
the moment
I realized
I was standing
right in front of you

and your hands
were at your sides.

I am standing on the shore
and I don't know how else to tell you
that I don't know what you want.
My feet are sunk deep in the sand and
doubt is a tide, rising.
I think you are somewhere on the horizon,
but I am too far down to see.
Fear weighs at my legs and claws at my lungs
and all I want to do is run,
but the sea is unforgiving and
the waves are getting closer.
I think that I am drowning when
I remember the way you smiled
(like maybe you wanted me to swim)
and, for a moment,
I convince myself I can breathe.
I tell myself I am capable of building ships
big enough to carry me to you.
And if I can't, let this body be a ship;
let this hope be its own tide.
But doubt still tastes like salt
running through an hourglass.
I am caught somewhere
between sails and flight
and, still,
the water is rising.

If you are
asking me
what I want,

it's this.
it's you.

What heartbreak it is,
to love those
who have built homes
in places you cannot.
No matter what country I am in,
there is someone missing from me.

Still, in an effort to be closer to you,
I drive to the sea.

Maybe I'm just afraid
that I will wrap my hands
around yours
and there will
still be oceans;
there will still be miles.

We step back, say,
"This is the line in the sand";
watch as the tide
strips it away.
know that we feel
the same way.

Now, I am
cutting ties;
letting go;
abandoning a ship
long after
it has sunk me.

This is
a goodbye.

I am trying to write it
like it is beautiful,
but it is sharp
at the edges
and I do not
understand it
at all.

I wish I could tell you how
I stood on a New York street
with the wind biting at me;
my phone was pressed
against my face
and I kept saying
your name.

I wish I had told you
I would have missed my flight.
I should have gotten back on a bus.
I would have found a way to stay.

Instead, I tell the night that
since I left you
nothing felt right.

I don't know how
to speak now
without the sound
of an
"I miss you"
buried
in the back
of my throat.

and I don't know how
you still don't hear it.

They ask me why
I didn't kiss you
goodbye.

I tell them
I would not have known
how to leave.

I think, in time, missing you
will become second nature.
I will sleep
without your scent
tangled in my hair; will not
dream of you, or wake up
and trace your outline
in the sheets beside me.

every dream I had with you
will spread behind us
like road maps of possibility
and, now, we will not grieve
that none of them
led us home.

It's just like swimming, they say.
Only I start to struggle, and I panic.
There is too much water and, beneath it,
too much space resting comfortably on
too much sand. And as hard as I fight it,
I am still sure that I am the thing
that is too much.

They will ask me what I am passionate about
and I will speak of the animals. the earth. the stars.
you. above all else,
you.

I want to believe
if I had more time.
less distance.

things would have been different.
the ending would not have come
when it did. life would have
held us longer. softer. with
some sort of gentleness
we never understood before.
we would have laughed. fallen
a little further in love.
lived so deeply that
regret never found us
and heartbreak happened
so slowly that
we could have been ready
to let go
as an act of nature
and not regret.

(the truth is that

any ending with you
would have been too soon.)

Somewhere
there probably exists
a version of me
that never knew you.

I have no desire to meet her.

We touch, with
no idea
of holding,

and I say
it is okay,
but
there is forever
on my breath;
there is always
on my hands.

And I know you are
just a moment.

When I think about you,
instinct tells me to pack a bag
and not include you in it.
To run until my lungs give out
and collapse against the tarmac
of a runway
that belongs to a place
that does not know me.
Breathe and breathe and breathe
but only carry a life that
is so consumed by newness
it does not understand
what it is like
to have had
and lost you.

Today, everything looks like
a green light.
Everything is telling me
to go.

I am leaving today.
carefully. strategically. meticulously.
I do not pack the grief.

still, it finds its way in.

like an unwrapped candy stuck in the pocket
of an old pair of jeans.
a receipt sent through the wash
and pulled apart through my suitcase,
plastering itself against fabric and
reminding me of a cost I am trying to forget.

but this life is brand new, isn't it?
it has never known or lost you.
this is a different country. a new city.
friends who never smiled at me
while I was talking about you.
but I am here. and I think
it doesn't matter.

because, still. *still.*
there is the grief.

You can tell
a lot
about a person
by the things
they run from
and the person
they run to.

I could say that I'm sorry.
gather the days I've spent missing you
and plant them like seeds
in the field behind my house.
water them with apology. tell them
I should have gone to you sooner.
held you longer. made less mistakes.

I sit amongst them and remember
that patience is a virtue
and it will grow only if I do;
watch the sunlight touch the earth
and pray they are better
at reaching for what they want
than I am.

and if not,
pray you will forgive me.

I try to write poems about
when love was a quiet thing.
when it had not touched me
or broken skin.

but it is difficult
to find anything beautiful
in the space before
I knew what it was
to love you.

My heart splits
somewhere down the middle
and an ocean floods in.
I grow around it.
The moon shifts the water inside me and
I wrap fiercely around something untamed.
somehow find space for the changing tides.
the rise and fall.
the unapologetic crash.
for the infinite sea.

You were standing
by the sea
and I was thinking
how
maybe you wanted
water at your feet

and I was a tidal wave.

Doubt traces the footfalls of a hello
and we try not to notice. we close the door.
tuck it shut, tightly. do not make eye contact
with the gap between the floor.
Love draws closer and (like a light)
the shadow is cast longer.

We adjust. angle ourselves away.
turn our faces to the light
like flowers at dawn and
convince each other that
there is anything romantic about frostbitten fingers.

We argue because
as hard as we have tried,
we have not yet learned to bite back words
the way we should.
Which is to say,
all the wrong things come out
in ways neither one of us can understand
and, like a sword,
we see the flash of teeth.
Explaining ourselves only serves as
a shackles-raised defense
and staying silent is not an option.
And sometimes this means
we are so afraid of miscommunication
that we do not speak at all.
Our differences pile between us
And, for a moment,
we forget they are beautiful.

I write you a poem
with every ounce of surrender.
of white flag.
of *we are on the same side.*
of *this was never a war.*

One moment it was
mountain breeze
between my lips and your skin
and then you left
with all the clean air.

I did not have a moment
to catch my breath
before I had to watch you
lose yours
over someone else.

I run circles around the same poem
and, like a desire to let go,
I cannot seem to find it.
It speaks of promise; a new life;
adventures I could have had with
a girl who did not want me.
I try to forgive us both for that;
try to tuck more than loss
between the pages; fold only the corners
of memories I want to keep
and, somehow,
still fold all of them.
What I mean to say is,
a life unlived is a treacherous thing.
I wanted to live mine with you.

This is not that poem.

My nature is open. forgiving. second chances
piled against thirds. I am soft.
I hold strength with both hands.
I only keep intimate relationships.
safe spaces as a consequence of
an almost unbearable vulnerability.
someone asks me how I feel
and an ocean spills from my lungs.
a girl laughs on a quiet street
and I don't know how to speak
without
cracking my chest open.

If I could close
the distance
between us
with
the miles
(the hours)
spent
running circles
around you
in my head,

there wouldn't
be any left.

There is beauty and romance in distance,
but, even with this, I can't romanticize it.
It demands you learn and put faith in timing and patience
and robs you of the ability to be a casual connection.
Distance lives in every relationship I hold
and I cannot help but warp my life around the water.

Hold the compass in your hands and understand
that you are the captain and not the sea.
Find a way to be with them. If you can't, make a plan.
call. keep communicating. write a letter, or a poem.
sing them a song. fill the space
until the day you don't have to.
Distance is hard, but it's harder when you don't know
when it will end, and it is almost impossible
when you don't know what you want.

We are love letters
lost at sea;
words distorted
and stripped away
by distance;
excuses washed up
like empty bottles
on our shores.

I think you did not feel me
wrap my heart around you
like a planet falling into orbit;
like a hope buried
in the spaces between fingers;
like quiet mornings
between sheets and longing
and an absolute fullness
of you.
and now I don't know how to tell you.
I don't know how to teach you
all the things
I always thought you knew.

I miss you because
I want to know how your day was.
what adventures you have been having.
what your life has looked like
since I left.

Mostly, I miss you because
I want to be a part of it.

I hope you know how
tentative
this strength can be;

how some days
I have to fight
harder and harder and
harder
not to reach for you
at all.

Maybe I am just afraid
that I will spend my whole life
dropping things
in favor of you
and one day
I will look down
and realize that
the floor is covered
in broken things
and I
am one of them.

The seasons change
and take you with them
and I press a summer stone
against my skin.

Autumn is here
and didn't bring you
home to me
and I hold it tighter
in my palm to keep it warm.

Winter comes
and bites all the same,
but in my hand
there is one last drop
of sunlight.
There is one last piece
of you.

I almost bought a plane ticket
when she left. I thought,
maybe things would have been
different, if I could have
just held her.
planted my feet in the earth
in front of her and
promised that would be
where I'd grow.

With us, trouble was a weed in the garden.
too tall. not enough leaves.
dug up. pulled. poisoned.
still there in the morning.
We planted flowers
hoping they would distract us.
painted the fence. again, and again.
tried to make it a joke.
a song sung at bedtime.
a laugh over breakfast.

Somehow, it spread.

We try to wipe it out, but
instead the earth is salted.
We watch our flowers wilt
against the weeds
through the kitchen window.
It is quiet. We do not laugh.
We plant the same seeds and
go to bed at war with the garden.
pretend the other is not watering it.
The distractions run dry.
Nobody sings.

I want to tell you this in a way
you will understand.
I am constantly moving, and
I wish you were with me.

I am somewhere so beautiful
and I turn as if you are there.
I am in the back of a taxi
winding through New York City;
I remember the way you held me
and an echo falls against my skin.
I have carried you with me and
written you into every memory I have made.

I imagine you
in every
empty seat
I sit beside.

The truth is that
when I imagined
my life
without you,
I put it down
and walked away.

There were suitcases
and highways
and planes
and runways.

Me, with
an inescapable
absence
of you.

I wish I could tell you
distance was the thing
that kept us apart;
smile over stories
of faces
I have crossed oceans to see
and how, after all this time,
they came home
to me.

But I have traveled
more times than I can count
to the cities of people
who could not open
their front doors
for me.

I blamed an ocean,
so I crossed it

(hands like waves)
(heart like anchor)

but planes cannot close
all distances,
and words cannot sustain
all sails.

I lie in bed with the people
I love most in this world.

I try to forget you used to be one of them.

For whatever reason,
you didn't reach for me.
I tell myself that you were scared.
There was too little time. too much.
It did not fit us the way
we thought it could. Summer rolled
into winter before we even noticed
the leaves change.
There was frost on the windows and
you tried to smile. But I did not see.
I was busy lining my pockets
with sacrifice and, besides,
you were nowhere near me.
I could say that there was someone else.
Tell you about lovers I have known who,
despite it all, did not know
how to choose me, either.
And even then, I did not
hold it against them. So,

I tell you I forgive you.

And I think
you understand.

I think
there will always be
an ache
in my heart
for you.

something
that reaches.

To every girl I can't be with,

I hope they hold you like you are every miracle they ever prayed for.
I hope you are loved with an almost unbearable tenderness.
understood more intimately
than I was ever capable of understanding you.
I hope you still see beauty in the way that I tried.

I understand that lifelines are not always woven
the way we think they should be and, my god,
I hope you are crossed with one that runs to the end of your days.
I hope they are long. full of joy. that the hardships do not break you.
and if they do, that you have someone beside you while you heal.

For you, I would have been a promise unfolding.
but I was one you could not make. or keep.
for whatever reason, I was not the story
you needed to write. my bones did not carry a life
the way you needed to live one. for that, I am sorry.
and, yet, not at all.

I want to thank you for loving me while you could.
for understanding that I was not right for you
even if I was not ready to accept it.
our lives were meant for great and beautiful things.
this was one of them.

There is a place in my heart that exists just for you.
I will protect it with my life.
hold you in my chest instead of my arms.
believe, in all sincerity, that this is enough.

I hope you know

just as much as I'm telling you
that I want it to be me,
I understand if it can't be.

I loved in a way
that knit eyebrows
above worried expressions
and cast concerned looks
across rooms filled
with serious, sit-down
conversations
with people who were just
trying to understand.

I loved in a way
that didn't fit
into a circle or a box
and oftentimes
didn't fit with you.

I loved in a way
that broke bubbles
and boundaries
and no hearts
but my own.

I trust that
everything
meant for us
has its time.
so,

it's okay
if this isn't ours.

I have talked myself
out of you
so many times
and, still,
it must mean something
that I never
had to talk myself
in.

I have always been the girl
with a plane ticket.
I have never known how to put my bags down
and not pick them back up.
I woke up one day with an understanding
that my heart was on either side of an ocean
and I began to live accordingly.
I sacrificed more than I can ever say;
put every cent I could into getting across the water;
grieved the things I would miss on either side.
This is to say, I have dedicated my life to love.

I did not realize how intimately tied
to my sense of identity and purpose
this had grown
until I lost the ability to travel;
until patrol officers put me on a canvas bed
and closed the border to my second home.

When I think about this soft, loyal thing in my chest,
I realize the truth is that this is the only life
that makes sense to me—
prioritizing the people I love
and doing everything I can to be with them
is the only thing that makes sense to me.
For me, the way home is paved
with the pages of a passport.

Let me be clear:
it has been unexplainably difficult.
it has carried so much heartbreak
but unquestionable joy.

I had never (not once) needed someone
to meet me halfway
or make the same sacrifices I had,
and when I was no longer capable of doing so,
I knew there would be relationships lost.
I did not know how difficult that would be.

I would still tell you with my dying breath
that love is a risk worth taking.

when I was seventeen, a career counselor
asked me what I wanted to do with my life
and what I wanted to be, and I told her,
"I just want to find new ways to love people."
every single flight I have taken
has been an act of love.
every single poem I've written
has been the same.

I throw a bottle out to sea.
I wait (and wait and wait)
for you to come back to me.

I try to write a love letter to distance
without begging it to return
the grace it once stole.
I try not to blame it
for the things I have lost;
for the bottles I threw out to sea
that never came back to me.
but my hands are shaking
and you're not here.
the ink is sinking through the pages
faster than I can write
and I wish I could blame distance,
but maybe these are faultless waters.

I try to write a new letter
and fill it with stories
about the times I crossed the world
to touch your face.
I know you are far away now
and even if I never do again,
I thank distance
for holding you at all.

The problem is not
that there is an anchor.

It's that
there's a chain.

Part of the reason
love is so complicated
is that
even when it's good—
especially when it's good—
it still destroys you,

and some people
just can't tell
the difference
between a love so good
it splits you open
and a love so bad
it tears you apart.

I understand that
there are oceans
spilled between us;
that sometimes miles
feel like eternities
and I am claimed
by foreign lands.
I understand if
distance unfolds
and no matter how many times
I promise to cross it,
you do not want it at all.

But I hope you understand
that if you decide you do,
there is nothing in this world
that would keep me
from you.

I wrote her a love letter after she left.
it said, "I hope you find what you're looking for.
I'm sorry it couldn't be me."

Now I write love letters to the things I am looking for.

Travel has saved me more times than I can count.
than is safe to admit. than anything else ever has,
other than love.
I wake up in a foreign city
and I am reminded that there is still new life.
new adventures. new faces to love,
other than hers.
these streets are a new story. this new world
hasn't lost anything of mine.
I never lived here before the grief.
it never knew you.

I step off the plane with the people
I love most in any world
and it is a new day. it is consumed with possibility.
it reeks only of things to be found.

(it whispers through the rain
that I will be one of them.)

a home for an ocean

fate. finding you. falling into place.

Let it be said
that I carried
just enough fear
for courage;
that I followed
an ache
in my heart;
that I smiled at you
like I was
never afraid;
that I understood
the gravity
of your hands
and I
reached
anyway.

I am sorry for the times
love did not hold you
the way you hoped it would

but when you're lying in my arms,
I am trying to say,
"I could."

I hear people talk about fate
like it will come easy.
find them without sacrifice—
without fear, or courage, or hard work.

I want to tell them
that I have looked fate in the eye
and it never (not once) came easy.
that it opened a door;
pointed me in the right direction;
smiled against the horizon and,
without apology,
demanded everything I had.

I hear people talk about fate
like it will come easy and,
for them, I wonder
if it will come at all.

I remember my grandmother
lying in a hospital bed
telling us about the colors in our heads,
how they find their way into your life
as you grow older.
She talks between curse words,
but when my grandfather calls
she smiles and I think,
maybe he is her color.

A year later
my best friend talks about
where the colors live,
how they build homes in the mess.

and I smile because
she is mine.

See? I have carried you
gently,
even when you did not
know how
to be held.
When you were sharp teeth
sunk deep
in soft flesh
and I ran my fingers
against your face
and told you
it was okay—

I understood that
fear was a buried instinct

and what were
a few more scars
anyway?

Quietly, and without meaning to,
I know you found safety here.
You were scared. The world did not know
how to hold you the way you thought it could
and, despite its best efforts,
you did not feel wanted.
You came to me speaking of storms
and I built you shelters, praying
you would find a home.
You did not come to build them with me,
but I held you too gently
and, here, fear was not a welcome mat.
Rain fell softly against the roof;
rolled peacefully down,
like hands on skin;
and, almost recklessly, you loved me
a little more than you planned to.

Maybe we were all wild
once.
maybe the world felt
less like an in-between
and more like a home.
maybe holding a hand
was less survival
and more hope.
maybe we were not afraid
of the way our skies
spill
into oblivion.
maybe we knew
we did not need to
ask permission
to live

(once)

The air is thick
and changing.
The leaves curl against a new season
and, for the first time,
we do not watch.
A new life is busy blooming;
there are hands to be held
and adventures to be had
and what is the night air, anyway,
if not just a space
to breathe with you?

My lungs are full and
I am breathless.
The season passes by
like a background
and
I am watching
you.

If I think about it too long,
you are everything I wanted.
I have stacked my life into columns
more times than I can count
and, still, have only seen colors.
What I mean to say is,
it has never made much sense.
I could choose just about anything,
and it would still fit my life like a misshapen sweater.
I could pull it on in the dead of winter,
and it would still itch.
But it is cold and you are smiling
and all I see is color.

My life piles up. breaks down.
and it all makes sense.

Mostly, I tell them
that you were built
on the bones
of compassion;
that there is an
almost unbearable
softness;
that there is light
buried in your hands.
I tell them
that I see romances
blooming
beneath your skin
and I can think of
one hundred ways
to unearth them.

(and that you exist.
you exist, you exist.)

One day, the bands we once listened to
will have all broken up. The coffee shops
we spent slow Sundays in will close their doors
and will have long since forgotten our names.
A song will start playing in the car
as we drive past the For Sale signs
on a street we once lived on
and, almost instinctively,
something inside us refuses to forget.

I reach for her with embers in my hands
and nothing but the promise of a slow burn.
I take time to touch her; breathe against her skin
and feed the flame.
we are careful. guarded.
we trace the scars from old lovers
who did not know how to hold us
and pray the future does.
it is soft. tender. more certainty
than we have ever known.
hope spreads like wildfire
and I try to stay grounded.
she laughs and I am reckless.
I tell her this heart
is less of a shelter
and more of a home;
take the locks off the doors
one by one.

she holds me under soft Fiji rain.
I try not to love her for that.

I got three new tattoos after a breakup
and, when the questions came,
I said,
"My heart will always carry
the people I have loved.
Why shouldn't my body
do the same?"

In this way. *In this small way.* We are still a forever.

I have given love
every chance
I've ever had.

I won't spend
a moment
of my life
regretting that.

Something we could not explain
if we had a thousand lifetimes
pulled us to this place
and, without thinking,
we collide.
For a moment, it is just us.
Everything is sudden bright-fire
and we try not to care
that the ashes fall against the skin
of other people.

With you, everything is soft
and so beautifully open
and, for a moment,
we tell ourselves we are safe.

I try to be friends with you and
move into an abandoned house.

I stand in front of what's left of it,
and I say,
"Love does not live here anymore."

but I remember that we used to,
and I think, this was once a home.
once, we planted flowers in the garden; lined pebbles
down the walkway; drank lemonade on the front porch.
here, I begged you to choose me,
and the word *almost*
echoed down the hallway
like a war cry that
almost made you stay.
the paint chipped. the walls ached. we lay quiet.
someone knocked at the door and we did not answer.
a layer of dust settled against the skin of our life,
and you left with all the clean air. I wilted
for as long as I could bear,
and then the house was empty.

a sign hammered into the garden out front
says it's set for demolition.
I remember the way you laughed
and I raise a sign in protest.

I say,
"Love does not live here anymore.
but
I do."

It was everything
I wanted.

I will spend my life
grateful
for the time
it was mine.

You ask me what
my favorite part
of all of it has been
and I could tell you
about a concert I went to.
a convention. queens.
friends, and the way
the leaves have changed.

But it is you.
it will always
be you.

Even though you are an ocean,
you could pour yourself out
and there would still be
some people
who would see nothing
but a half-empty cup of sand.

The right love for you will hold you like a certainty.
come to you in ways you never imagined and
never (not once) make you feel like
you cannot find the balance
between too much
and not enough.

I want to believe
you loved me; that

in some part of your heart,
you still do.

Touch me
like a story
you have always
wanted
to tell.

Love me
like a promise
you know
you can keep.

I try to get better at letting go.
a girl walks out and I don't understand why
and I try not to go outside to
trace her footsteps in the snow.
I try not to pull the door from the hinges.
I tend the fire. sweep the floors. keep the smell of her
in my sheets. tangle it in my hair.
take our pictures off the walls and
tell myself it's still a home.
fall asleep without her and swear to myself
it's still a home.

Someday,
I will hear a girl laugh
and it will sound something like you
and it won't be met with an ache in my heart.

the leaves will change color
without a thought of you. I will dye my hair
and try to do the same.

Someday,
I will heal enough to hold a dream
that never knew your name. reach boldly,
knowing it was only ever meant to be mine.

people will speak of the love in your life
and my hands won't feel empty. the future
will unfold like a miracle and I won't
wish you were a part of it.

Someday,
I will meet someone with your smile
and walk the other way.

We had the kind of love
where I held so tight
you burned me
and, still, when
I looked at my hands
and my burned-off fingerprints,
I thanked you
for the reminder:

holding on to you
is not worth
losing me.

I stack my heartbreaks up
next to each other
more times than I care to admit.
the shrapnel lines up, but
someone did not stay
to pull pieces with me.
someone did.
I look at them this way, and I think,
how did you hold me when I was healing?
what did that look like? could you even bear
to look at the battleground when it was over?
did shame cover your eyes like a babe
terrified of the dark? or were you brave enough
to look me in the eye? did the promise of forever
spin out like red yarn across the ground;
was love a white flag in the wind,
or was it a victory, even in the end?

You are poetry
even when nobody
is writing it down.

I don't know what I imagined it would be like.
I don't think it was this.
It was almost two years before we were in the same place
and nothing could have prepared me.

A church door sits ajar and
we almost pass right by,
but you run inside
and, suddenly, it is a place of worship.

We follow a man who carries a lantern;
he talks about the things that haunt us,
and as we stand in a small graveyard,
you teach me a lesson in energy.
I make a joke:

you laugh and the universe cracks open.

The shop windows are lit
along a street in Virginia.
Someone plays an accordion
and I hold your hand.
What I am trying to say is that
you put a few bills
into the case of a saxophone
and this is what I mean
by oblivion.

I know there is
an ache
in your heart.
I see it,
feel it,
intimately understand it.
And it does not scare me.

Let me be clear:
you do not scare me.

I am exhausting the possibility
that there are more poems
to be written
about the day we met.
I have folded them
with heavy hands
through these pages
and I still think
there is so much more to say.

Give me more days,
I say.

Stay.

There are entire worlds
built for us here.
This is the place where
I know you can stay
and I do not have
to keep our story
a secret.
I do not think
you will ever read it,
but if you do,
know that this is not
a prison
for regret.
I have let you go
in every way
I know how.

And, yet,
not at all.

You see, it is a hill and a valley.
and no breathing thing knows how to stay still.
we climb, and it is laborious.
our legs grow weary, but we press on.
we understand that we are forging our own path
and nobody will see it the way we do.
the air thins, and at the crest
nothing is more beautiful.
we are together
and the universe takes a breath.
but it cannot last forever,
do you understand?
you are here, and then you are not.
the descent is an exhale.
we pause at a river
to catch our breath
and write stories about the hilltop.
bind them in books.
sit around campfires in the valley
and fall in love with the peace
of knowing one does not exist
without the other.

This soft thing in my chest.

This time, I will give it only
to someone who reaches
with certainty; who understands
the nature of gentle hands.
I will not be a secret.
I will not be a home for doubt.
I will wait for the girl
who carries patience like a prayer
and smiles at me like maybe
I am a reawakening of joy.
and I will love her
like rain is not a reason
for shut doors but
a cause for celebration.

The truth is that it isn't hard to choose someone.
The people you truly want
hardly feel like a choice at all.
It is a gravity, nothing less.

Once, I could not stop moving because
I couldn't bear to look at the solid line between
what I wanted and what wanted me.
I did not realize it was a distance I was trying to cross alone.
It filled up with doubt. with grief. with more and more and
more distance. the kind that has nothing to do with
where you are and everything to do with
whether it feels like it matters
where you are.

I want to hold the world accountable
for the times it could have touched you gently
but did not.
I would speak in hushed tones
of violences against you
and wash them harshly
from the truth;
write a new story for you,
full of happy endings
and bereft of grief;
send soft-handed lovers
of every kind
to be with you
when comfort evaded you
and, in some small way,
make sadness a stranger again.

But even if I could,
who am I to change your story?

When the world overwhelms me
in a darkened-brow
kind of way
and my restless soul
is emboldened by a map
and a need to disappear,
I hope my fleeting feet
find you
around every corner—
not because you have been
waiting on the curb
but because
my compass heart
doesn't point north;
it points home.

I just hope
there's
a part of you
that only
breathes
when you
see me.

If you're trying to figure out
how you feel about someone,

imagine that
they're walking down the street in a year
and they're holding hands with the person
they love most in the world.

Now imagine that it's not you.

I will admit that I have called myself hard to date
when I should have said
I don't know how to be a casual thing
and sometimes that means
I don't know how to be something that doesn't scare you.
I should have said I am still learning not to apologize for it.
what I should have said is that
I know how to be something that holds you.
makes you laugh. folds adventure through your life like silk.
puts you first with infinite patience. reminds you that you are
worthy of it all.
I should have said that distance wears the face of an ocean,
but I want you to come with me.
that ease does not equate worth. that
everything is hard if you don't know what you want.
that love is a risk. that all the best things are.
I should have said that I am not afraid
of anything inside you. that I will love you fiercely.
find poetry in your hands on a quiet Tuesday.
open to you like a flower in June.
that I know how to be the softest thing in the universe
to you. a prayer whispered in early morning light.
soft petal rain. something that reaches for you.
builds a life out of a dream and
doesn't look back. chooses you. never tires of you.
craves to know you the way the sky does.
says your name in their sleep. keeps you safe.
throws you into the wind but catches you. and catches you and.
catches you.

I should have said that I'm worth it.

Maybe, in time,
I will unlearn you.

Maybe
your voice won't
wrap around my name
like my favorite song.
your nose won't crinkle
in my memory
like a shirt I can't take off.
you will laugh
and I won't hear it
and the room won't flood
with clean air.

Maybe the station will change.
a new song will find me. new hands
will hold mine, and I will not for a moment
miss yours.

Maybe, in time,
I will unlearn you.
but I hope I don't have to.

I think, in time, you will be a jar on the shelf.
a small box of memories in a very large house.
a beautiful work of art in an ever-expanding gallery.
I will stop to admire you sometimes.
perhaps more often than I would like;
than is healthy for me; than people would advise.
but I will not pause too long.
you are a dream into which I poured
everything I thought I had, and then some.
I am constantly in danger of gluing my feet
to the floor in front of you.
but, like all breathing things,
I know the stillness would kill me.
and you—moving like butterfly wings—
are no longer here.
I peel myself away. buy more jars and fill them with new memories.
put the box inside another box.
close your wing of the gallery on weekends.
tell myself that this small infinity
is enough.

I met her in a bar
in the East Village of New York City
and, like gravity,
something inside me fell into place.

I began to learn her over teacups of vodka,
pouring secrets to one another
as we stood against red-carpet walls.
I heard her read poetry for the first time
and it was a song sung from someplace familiar.
(I have listened for it every day since.)
she was soft curls and lullaby lips
and more grace than I could imagine.

Maybe everything doesn't come down to voice memos
at midnight; can't be counted by
the months I spent missing her
or the ones by her side. but she held my hand and
I learned a lesson in family.
I learned another when I saw her face
in those of her children.
I split my life across an ocean and, still,
coming back to her feels like coming home. still,
something about the way she laughs
tells me I had been searching for something
all my life
and this was it. this was it and she was it
and I am never letting her go.

(still, when someone asks me
about miracles,
I tell them about you.)

For you,
I will be a shelter of bones;
an unbroken promise
in a sea of falsehoods.
I will catch the waves
against my skin
and not let any water in;
wrap the softest words
around you and
never ask you
to apologize
for the days
you are the storm.

The things I lost along the way
didn't stop me
from having dreams,
and now they're coming true.

All I want
is for you to believe
yours can, too.

I wake up every morning
and lend my voice to love.

I lie awake at night
sure
there is still so much more
to say.

A girl put the smile back on my face.
She thinks it's weird I sometimes watch her sleep.
I don't know how to explain
that when the night falls down around us like a heavy blanket
and the light across the street filters through the blinds
to find her skin, her face holds
every ounce of softness; of tenderness; of intimacy
I can imagine.

She laughs and buries her face
when I tell her she reaches for me in her sleep.
I don't tell her that when she sleeps,
all the romanticism of a sunflower field
tucks itself sweetly into the corners of her mouth
like it is waiting for the day to break
before it can bloom against mine.
I kiss her face and pull her closer.
I don't tell her that I think about it,
again again again.

All of this is to say,
when she sleeps next to me,
I lie awake and dream of her.

Everything is bright and new and
uncertain. I tell her,
"Love is a risk."

Doors are opened without being
torn from the hinges.
wildfire licks our skin
without leaving a mark.

I bury hope
in the crook of my elbow;
in her dimples; in my scars.
I count my blessings
none of them
are her work.

And when she talks about risks
now
she tells me
I was one worth taking.

a dangerous smile. a wild hunger.
hands the color of deadly nightshade.
a berry rolled between lips.
a small amount of pressure. your skin.
teeth that puncture. sweetly.
brush against the flesh of the fruit.
do not notice the poison
until long after it has traced my chin;
stained my fingers;
gathered in the hollow of my neck.

I add your name
to the list of things
I survived this year.

note it: barely.

Here in this room,
I am learning the shape of your mouth
when it softens against the morning light.

I am learning the sound of your laugh
curling through the night air
and I hold my breath
like
it will somehow make the gift of this lesson
last
just a little bit longer.

And, here,
the sheets find the unique shape of us;
find the smell of you tangled in my hair;
find the almost unbearable tenderness
of your skin against mine.

Here, I hold your face in my hands
and they have never felt more full.
here,
confetti scatters across the bed
like it's celebrating the fact
you were ever here at all.

I don't want
anything
from you.

just everything
with you.

There are
poems
against my skin;
all the places you have been.

I press my mouth
against the gunpowder of skin

my tongue rolls
like a match

your back
arches like a smoke signal

there is less
and less air
and yet

there is wildfire.

I am a fleeting thing,

but you reach for me
and I have never been
so intimately
acquainted
with the desire
to stay.

I have always been called
too much; too intense.
You are a lesson that
their words were only ever
an unmet need.
And this is a home
for an ocean.
This is a wanting
in equal measure.
This is sunlight
between two flowers
opening.
This is the way
you look at everything inside me
and say you are not afraid.

I lay my head
upon
the rise and fall
of the chest
of faith.

I graze my teeth
above
the underbelly
of surrender.

Hope is a breath
in the night.
It carries the voice
of fate.

I will hold you
with harbor arms.

the lighthouse
finding a ship
against the lonely sea.
a shelter
as your legs give out
under torrential rain.

what I am trying to tell you is,
you are safe here.

They ask me
about love
and, for
the first time,
I think about you.

We say forever
and pray this time it's true.

To the girl I belong with,

You are the miracle I have waited my whole life
to happen to me. I have searched the world over
to find you; in some unexplainable and exquisite way,
have carried you with me and written about you long before
I could ever write about you.
I have wanted only a love that does not fall asleep
hungry
for something else; a love that knows it is mine
the second
I walk through the door. I will not settle for anything less
than the way I feel when I look at you.
I am grateful (in a way I never thought I would be)
for the endings that came before you.
When I find you (if I don't already hold you),
know that
your heart can stay in your chest and still be held in my hands.
know that we will be safe. tender. kinder and more adventurous
than we have ever known.
we will be home.

On my good days,
I speak in riddles about fate.
I say if I have run circles around
this feeling
just trying to find logic
and never reached the center,
the answer must be fate.
and it makes sense, doesn't it?
when I tell you
you are the only thing in my life
that I can't explain,
what I'm trying to say is,
I think this word belongs to you.

If there is a gravity
inside me
(which there is),
if there are universes
and constellations
and a quiet oblivion
(which there are),

loving you
needs no explanation.
Losing you needs no explanation.
The push and pull
of knowing you
needs no explanation.

It is a breath.
It is an eternity.

Today, someone told me I am going to hell
for loving you.
Yesterday, they did not realize
I was writing about a girl,
but today? today they say
those words are going to burn with me.

I don't know what to say about this
except that when you laugh,
I understand the need for churches.
you hold me like a confessional, and I tell you that
we have known demons, but you were never one of them.
I tell you, it is a miracle we got this far.
I did not know light before I saw it
pouring through your stained-glass heart,
but sunlight hits your skin like a prayer,
and I promise to be a sanctuary for joy.
and this is worship, isn't it? this is faith.
I watch you wake up on a Sunday morning,
and I am not afraid to die, because
every time I fall in love, I catch a glimpse of heaven.

And, loving you?
Oh, it would be
a sin
not to.

If they stare
(which they might),
knot your fingers in mine and
do not think of white flags.
If they talk
(which they will),
tell them that this love
didn't come easy;
how it rained on that night
when we couldn't sit still.
And even
if it hurts us
(which it could),

know that I am not afraid
to hold your hand.

As big and beautiful and consuming
as my love for travel is,
there is an equal part of me
that belongs to my country.
to my home. to the arrow through my heart.
to the people and the places
that have built and grown me,
from the beginning.

For the first time,
I have allowed myself
to find love
on my own shores.
It is more safety than the loves that lived
in any other country. It understands me,
speaks with the same cadence,
wants to meet my family, and
does not travel on gaslight flames.
It looks like sunflower fields.
tulip bouquets. Kombi vans parked
by our beaches.
It smells like her sweater in my bed.
sounds like her laugh in the darkness.
feels like home.

For as far
as I fell

I flew higher, still.

Gravity is an ebb and flow. One moment,
New York is calling me. I buy a flight. I pack my bags.
But my niece calls and when I answer the phone,
I think it is gravity pulling me home.

If I am being honest (which I am trying to be),
I do not think I know how to stay.
Half my heart is on either side of an ocean
and I am never sure which one to follow
but, almost recklessly, am in constant pursuit.
I call this a gravity; the way a place or a person
calls to us. holds us. pulls us in and out of place.
I smiled at a girl once and I think I felt it. the shift.
I saw the leaves in Central Park, and
New York has held a part of me ever since.
When I think about gravity—this unexplainable
and undeniable thing I carry inside me—
it feels a lot like fate.
the way she smiled back. my best friend's curly hair.
the sound of my niece laughing. my sister's jokes.
Montréal. gay bars in West Hollywood. a small village in eastern
Uganda.
places and moments that have held me without question
and never let me go.

It is a small rebellion,
don’t you think?

This bravery.

Love is a gravity.

Let it pull you
in the right direction
and you will fall
where you belong.

*Acknowledgments*

I have been honored with an incredible collection of people to write to and connect with, who have found me both online and in my personal life. This book would be incomplete without those who got me here.

The HeartMath Institute, whose work and ideas have changed my life. Amy and Evolette, who have always been my solid ground. My mother, my constant. Bailey, my guiding light and greatest belief in fate. Amy, who reawakened my hope. Alison, who found family with me. Courtney and James, who believed in this book. Hilary, who holds so much space in these pages. and Andrews McMeel Publishing for making this dream come true.

I cannot thank you enough,
but thank you.

Enjoy *The Gravity Inside Us* as an audiobook narrated by the author, wherever audiobooks are sold.